First World War
and Army of Occupation
War Diary
France, Belgium and Germany

59 DIVISION
177 Infantry Brigade
Durham Light Infantry
2/6th Battalion
10 January 1918 - 31 August 1919

WO95/3023/4

The Naval & Military Press Ltd
www.nmarchive.com
Published in association with The National Archives

Published by

The Naval & Military Press Ltd

Unit 10 Ridgewood Industrial Park,

Uckfield, East Sussex,

TN22 5QE England

Tel: +44 (0) 1825 749494

www.naval-military-press.com

www.nmarchive.com

This diary has been reprinted in facsimile from the original. Any imperfections are inevitably reproduced and the quality may fall short of modern type and cartographic standards.

© **Crown Copyright**
Images reproduced by permission of The National Archives, London, England, 2015.

Contents

Document type	Place/Title	Date From	Date To
Heading	WO95/3023/5 2/6 Battalion Durham Light Infantry		
Heading	59th 177th Infy Bde 2-6th Bn Durham Lt Infy May 1918-Aug 1919		
Heading	War Diary Of 2/6th Garrison Guard Bn Durham L.I. For The Month Of May 1918		
War Diary	Frinton On Sea	01/05/1918	06/05/1918
War Diary	Dover	06/05/1918	06/05/1918
War Diary	Balais	06/05/1918	07/05/1918
War Diary	Fonline Hes	08/05/1918	08/05/1918
War Diary	Bryas	08/05/1918	08/05/1918
War Diary	Pressy Les Pernes	09/05/1918	09/05/1918
War Diary	Le Vielfort	10/05/1918	31/05/1918
War Diary	Le Vielfort	10/01/1918	24/01/1918
Operation(al) Order(s)	2/6th G.G. Bn. Durham L.I.		
War Diary	War Diary Of 46th Garrison Battalion Durham Light Infantry For The Month Of June 1918		
War Diary	Le Vielfort	01/06/1918	09/06/1918
War Diary	Cambligneul	11/06/1918	15/06/1918
War Diary	Bois De Hazois	16/06/1918	16/06/1918
War Diary	Eps	17/06/1918	20/06/1918
War Diary	Reclinghem	22/06/1918	30/06/1918
Miscellaneous	2/6 Garrison Battalion Durham Light Infantry.		
Heading	War Diary Of The 2/6th Bn Durham L.I. For The Month Of July 1918.		
War Diary	Reclinghem	09/07/1918	09/07/1918
War Diary	Canlers	10/07/1918	24/07/1918
War Diary	Chatmaigre	25/07/1918	30/07/1918
Miscellaneous	2/6th Bn Durham L.I. Nominal Roll Of Offers.	31/07/1918	31/07/1918
Heading	War Diary Of The 2/6th Bn Durham Light Infantry For The Month Of August 1918.		
War Diary	Chat Maigre	01/08/1918	03/08/1918
War Diary	Bretencourt	04/08/1918	08/08/1918
War Diary	Gouy-En-Artois	11/08/1918	17/08/1918
War Diary	Mercatel	17/08/1918	23/08/1918
War Diary	Saucty	23/08/1918	23/08/1918
War Diary	Lambres	24/08/1918	24/08/1918
War Diary	St Venant	26/08/1918	26/08/1918
War Diary	Calonne	27/08/1918	28/08/1918
War Diary	L'epinette	30/08/1918	30/08/1918
War Diary	Near Lestrem	31/08/1918	31/08/1918
War Diary	River Laye Near Lestrem	01/09/1918	02/09/1918
War Diary	Robecq	03/09/1918	03/09/1918
War Diary	Paradis	05/09/1918	05/09/1918
War Diary	Fosse	07/09/1918	07/09/1918
War Diary	Riez Bailleul	09/09/1918	09/09/1918
War Diary	M17.c.5.4	13/09/1918	13/09/1918
War Diary	La Near Basse Rd	19/09/1918	19/09/1918
War Diary	Clifton. C,	22/09/1918	22/09/1918
War Diary	Post Nine Pin Trench	29/09/1918	29/09/1918
War Diary	Arrived		

War Diary	Near Aubers	01/10/1918	02/10/1918
War Diary	Lille Sector	03/10/1918	06/10/1918
War Diary	Croix Marechal	07/10/1918	07/10/1918
War Diary	Bas St Maur	10/10/1918	14/10/1918
War Diary	Croix Marechal	16/10/1918	16/10/1918
War Diary	Capinghem	17/10/1918	17/10/1918
War Diary	St Andre	18/10/1918	18/10/1918
War Diary	St Meurice	18/10/1918	18/10/1918
War Diary	Lille Sector	18/10/1918	18/10/1918
War Diary	Le. Recueil	19/10/1918	19/10/1918
War Diary	Touffleurs	20/10/1918	21/10/1918
War Diary	River Escaut	22/10/1918	22/10/1918
War Diary	Scheldt	22/10/1918	30/10/1918
War Diary	Hulans	31/10/1918	31/10/1918
Miscellaneous	Honours & Decorations		
War Diary	Hulans	01/11/1918	01/11/1918
War Diary	Nepinette (Hdgro)	03/11/1918	08/11/1918
War Diary	Toufflers	08/11/1918	10/11/1918
War Diary	Rumez	11/11/1918	11/11/1918
War Diary	Templeuve	12/11/1918	12/11/1918
War Diary	Ascq	15/11/1918	15/11/1918
War Diary	Seclin	16/11/1918	30/11/1918
Heading	War Diary Of The 2/6th Battalion The Durham Light Infantry For The Month Of December 1918		
War Diary	Seclin Near Lille	01/12/1918	03/12/1918
War Diary	Bracquemont	07/12/1918	03/01/1919
War Diary	St Martin Eglise Dieppe	15/01/1919	15/01/1919
Heading	War Diary For The Month Of February 1919		
War Diary	Martin Eglise Embaskarin Camp	01/02/1919	28/02/1919
Miscellaneous	2/6th. Bn. The Durham Light Infantry		
Heading	War Diary For The Month Of March 1919		
War Diary	Martin Eglise	01/03/1919	15/03/1919
War Diary	Beaulieu	15/03/1919	21/03/1919
War Diary	Calais	23/03/1919	31/03/1919
Heading	War Diary For The Month Of April. 1919		
War Diary	Calais	01/04/1919	30/04/1919
Heading	War Diary For The Month Of May 1919		
War Diary	Calais	01/05/1919	31/05/1919
War Diary	No. 7 Camp. Calais.	01/06/1919	30/06/1919
War Diary	Nos.H. 5and 8 Leave Camp Calais	01/07/1919	31/07/1919
War Diary	Vendroux	03/08/1919	31/08/1919

WO95/3023/5
2/6 Battalion Durham Light Infantry

59TH DIVISION
177TH INFY BDE

2-6TH BN DURHAM LT INFY
MAY 1918 – AUG 1919.

From UK

Vol 1

Confidential
War Diary
of
2/6th Garrison Guard Bn Durham L.I.
for the month of
May 1918.

WAR DIARY or INTELLIGENCE SUMMARY

2/6 Garrⁿ Guard Battalion. Durham Light Infantry

May 1918.

Army Form C. 2118.

Place	Date	Hour	Summary of Events and Information	Remarks and references to Appendices
Frinton on Sea	1.5.18		The unit, mobilized as a Garrison Battalion, is ready to proceed Overseas. War Establishment No 1937 Part VII S.D.2 dated 27.2.18. Authority W.O. Letter N°. 121/France/2044 (Mob 1) dated 18.4.18.	7B
do	5/6.5.18		Entrained at Frinton in three trains. 22.35, 23.10, 5.1.18. 03.30, 6.1.18. First two trains accommodating HeadQrs. & 4 Companies. Third train conveying Transport personnel, the latter proceeding via Southampton & the former via Dover. Strength. 37 Officers 1066 Other Ranks. 55 Animals. This figure includes 3 officers 96 Other Ranks as first Reinforcement.	7B
Dover	6.5.18	11.00	Embarked per S.S. "Golden Eagle" weather foggy.	7B
Calais	do	14.00	Disembarked. Route march to N° 2 Dieppe[?] Camp.	7B
do	7.5.18		All ranks T.Y.Q. Beaumaris. Reinforcements 3 off^s 96 o.R. proceeded to B.1 Personnel Base. Etaples. Authority. 3rd Echelon C T 269. Transport Section arrived having proceeded Southampton to Calais.	7B
Fontinettes	8.5.18	15.15	Marched to Fontinettes Station, entrained, authority, Q.L./1948/C/11. 251169 Serjeant R.E. Hague, O.R. Clerk, proceeded to A.G's Office, Rouen, for duty.	7B
Bryas	do	22.15	Arrived. Detrained 23.15. Route march to	7B
Pressy les Pernes	9.5.18	01.30	arrived.	7B

WAR DIARY or INTELLIGENCE SUMMARY

Army Form C. 2118.

2/6th Bn. Gd. Bn. Divch: L : 1

May, 1918

Place	Date	Hour	Summary of Events and Information	Remarks and references to Appendices
PRESSY LES PERNES	9.5.18	16.00	Route march to FAUX, embussed for LE VIELFORT HOUDAIN. Encamped. J26.b. 2.7	SHEET 36.B. 7/3
LE VIELFORT	10.5.18		Instructions received that the unit is in future to be known as 2/6th Garrison Guard Battalion. The Durham Light Infantry and is included in 177th Infantry Brigade, 59th Division, Xth Corps, 1st Army. Authority Xth Corps G/149/1/Q. & will be employed in preparing no 3 Sub section of Sector "A" of a line known as "B.B." Line. This consists of Front, Support & Reserve Lines & runs from I6.a. 4.6. to W27.d. 9.0	36.B.
			The portion allotted to this unit to prepare is from J7.d. 4.0 to J34.c. 5. 3.	do
			The portion allotted to this unit to hold in the event of necessity during process of construction is from J36.a. 5.0. to Bruay, St Pol Rd. J20.a.8.6. inclusive with Battalion Headquarters at J27.c. 6.0.	do 7/3
do	11.5.18		Task commenced. 6 hrs digging daily & thro training daily's except Sunday 08.30 to 13.00 Training.	7/3
do	31.5.18		Work proceeded without unusual occurrences from 11th to 31st in very good weather there only being 1 wet day (ie 24th inst.) This weather which had been particularly hot prior to that day, becoming a little cooler. The health of troops on the whole very satisfactory with only a small proportion of minor casualties.	7/3

WAR DIARY / INTELLIGENCE SUMMARY

Army Form C. 2118.

2/5th G.G.A. Durh. L.I.

May 1918

Place	Date	Hour	Summary of Events and Information	Remarks and references to Appendices
LE VIELFORT	10.1.18		251735. Cpl Aspinal G. to Hospital. V.D.H. Off Strength 17th June	7/8
do	11.1.18		252371 Pte Smith W.H. do do 18th June	7/8
do	12.1.18		2 men detached for duty 177 Bde.	7/8
do	do		3 " " R.E. (2 Driver. 1 Rifleman)	7/8
do	16.1.18		716/2 Pte Parkin. Hospital. Off Strength 23.1.18	7/8
do	17.1.18		251635 " Lynch D " " 24.1.18	7/8
do	17.1.18		267148 " Skinner A " " 24.1.18	
do	18.1.18		Capt H.B. Smith Rtnd. Hospital R.E. (2 Driver, 1 Rifleman)	7/8
do	18.1.18		Lieut J.S. Smellie + 12 NCOs men "C" Coy attached for duty CAUCHY-A-LA-TOUR	7/8
do	do		10 men attached for duty R.E. RE RECEIVED	
do	18.1.18		2 men " " " O.S.C. GAUCHIN LE GAL. MONCHY	7/8
do	19.1.18		9108 Pte Webster Hospital Broken ankle kicked from Horse. Off Strength 26.1.18	
			993980 " Kinealan G.A. do do 27.1.18	
			66513 " Baul. E. do do 29.1.18	
			80485 " Potter. H. do do	7/8
			99401 " McCafferty. J. do do	
do	24.1.18		12 NCOs proceeded to attend 59 Divl Lewis Gun Course. SAINS LES PERNES. Schoolman and Cook	
do	do		Lieut F. Williamson + 1 NCO proceeded to attend Course at 1st Army Musketry Sch. MATTRINGHEM.	
do	do		also taken as Batman. 99197 Pte Dabb. J. Hospital. Off Strength 31.5.18. Strength 31.5.18 Officers. Other Ranks.	7/8
			(including detached + N.C.O. + Drums Sgts.) 34. 960.	

Signed 2/O Durh L.I. (9th Gd An)

Lt. Col.

2/6th G.G.Bn.Durham L.I.

NOMINAL ROLL OF OFFICERS DOING DUTY WITH THE BATTALION.

Lieut.Col.J.Spain.
Captain G.Williams. (A/Major).
Captain T.Beddy.
Captain H.P.Hinde.
Captain W.H.C.Cooke.
Captain A.W.Lawton.
Captain G.R.Angus.
Lieut.C.J.A'Hern.
Lieut.A.Green.
Lieut.A.Cook.
Lieut.F.Copeland.
Lieut.L.C.A.Benson.
Lieut.W.G.Orriss.
Lieut.F.G.Browne.
Lieut.J.R.Wallace.
Lieut.A.W.Drabble.
Lieut.G.B.Howson.
Lieut.W.S.Macadam.
2nd Lt. H.F.Lucas.
2nd Lt.R.C.Montford.
2nd Lt.C.St.A.Ratcliffe.
2nd Lt.J.S.Willcox.
2nd Lt.R.L.Davis.
2nd Lt.L.H.Perry.
2nd Lt.R.Pratt.
2nd Lt.A.V.Blake.
2nd Lt.S.B.Hodgson.
2nd Lt.L.V.Hardy.
Hon.Capt.& Qr.Mr.W.B.Wiltshire.

Attached: Captain C.C.Boyle, R.A.M.C.

NOMINAL ROLL OF OFFICERS DETACHED.

Captain H.G.Smith Rowse - Hospital.
Lieut.J.E.Williamson.   - Course.
Lieut.H.V.Davis.   - Course.
2nd Lt. J.E.Smellie   - R.E. for duty.

31.5.18.

Lieut.Colonel,
Commanding,
2/6th G.G.Bn.Durham L.I.

Confidential.

War Diary
of
2/6th Garrison Battalion
Durham Light Infantry
for the month of
June 1918.

June 1918

WAR DIARY 2/6th Garr" Bn Suss. R.V.

INTELLIGENCE SUMMARY

(Erase heading not required.)

Army Form C. 2118.

Place	Date	Hour	Summary of Events and Information	Remarks and references to Appendices
LE VIEILFORT			Capt. Geo. Williams	
	1.6.18		2/Lt Almaix Walsh 2nd in Command dated 5.5.18. Gazette 21.5.18.	7B
	8.6.18		Revd H. Thomas arrival taking on strength.	7B
	9.6.18	6.P.b.f.f	heard work on B.B. line in HOUDAIN AREA. Divisional Practice. Marching B.B. Line. The unit took part in scheme & was explained the following	7B Sked
			order to defend - from road running approx. N. & S. through J.33 Central (inclusive) to the Line I.23. Somersets on the left. 17th Suff. Bde on the Right.	H.R. 3
			Central - Siege No 3 inclusive. 11th Somersets on the left. 176th Inf. Bde. on the Right.	1/WS 00
			Bn. Hadqs. J27.c.6.0. Bde. Hadqs. P.15.c.5.0.	7B
CAMBLIGNEUL	11.6.18		Proceeded from LE VIEILFORT by march route to CAMBLIGNEUL. Encamped W.21.d.47	7B
do	12.6.18		Rested.	7B
do	13.6.18		Commenced digging on B.B. Line. No 3 Sub sector SAVY. also on G.H.Q Line zwecking to	7B do
do	15.6.18		ceased work on B.B & G.H.Q Lines SAVY Sector	7B
Bois de Hazois	16.6.18		March Route to Bois de Hazois. J.35. d.4.8. Operation Order No 121. Encamped for night	7B
EPS	17.6.18		do do do EPS. G.32.a.8.9. Operation order No 122. Troops Billeted.	7B do
do	18/9			7B do
do	20.6.18		Reorganising in accordance with G.H.Q. Letter A.G. 4196 (0) dated 8.6.18.	7B
			Commenced training with a view to fitting the unit to take its place in a quiet sector of the Line. The Division having been detailed for this duty.	7B Div Letter 7/3 No 437/7 G
RECLINGHEM	22.6.18		Half the Battalion the Batt" completed its move into Divisional training area, proceeding by March Route to LAIRES & then by Motor Lorries to RECLINGHEM. The other half by motor Lorries to LAIRES & then Route March to RECLINGHEM	15.6.18 Sheet 36.D 76 Eastern Holt

Army Form C. 2118.

WAR DIARY
INTELLIGENCE SUMMARY.
(Erase heading not required.)

Instructions regarding War Diaries and Intelligence Summaries are contained in F. S. Regs., Part II. and the Staff Manual respectively. Title pages will be prepared in manuscript.

Place	Date	Hour	Summary of Events and Information	Remarks and references to Appendices
RECLINGHEM	JUNE 22nd		Battalion Billeted in Houses. Barns &c "B" Company being detached at LILETTE Q.27.b.	7/B 36.D Easter Map 1/40,000
			Bn Hdqrs. W.4ª.9.9.	
	22nd		LIEUT. QM.R. W.B. WILTSHIRE to be Hon Capt & Qmr. under A.C.I. 1351/17 with effect from 28th May 1918.	7/B
	23/30		Battalion engaged training as per programme issued by Brigade.	
			Weather very fine during month only 2 wet days.	7/B
			Casualties affecting Strength of Unit.	
	19/20		Med. Board by Inspector of Staff. Result. 1 raised to A. 100 Lowered to B.III. 14 Lowered to B.III. 7/B	
	May 2nd/29		Gazett. CAPT. H.G. SMITH REWSE. Last sustained Lieut struck off strength Einstern. Irck.	7/B
	24/5/18		Decrease. Increase.	7/B
	28/6/18		4. Hospital over 7 days. 1 rec'd. from Hosp?	7/B
			12 do do 4.6.18	7/B
				7/B
			1. Hosp: over 7 days 13.6.18 3 do	7/B
	20.6.18		71 to Labour Corps Base 6.6.18 8. Reinforcements	7/B
	21.6.18		12 Hosp: for 7 days 15.6.18 2 rec'd from Hosp!	7/B
	26.6.18		100. 20.6.18 38 Reinforcements	
			52	
			During the last 2 weeks of the month an epidemic of Spang Influenza broke out, affecting 10 officers & approx 500 other Ranks. about 400 of whom were attached to Field Hosp! for treatment.	7/B

Army Form C. 2118.

WAR DIARY
INTELLIGENCE SUMMARY.
(Erase heading not required.)

Instructions regarding War Diaries and Intelligence
Summaries are contained in F. S. Regs., Part II.
and the Staff Manual respectively. Title pages
will be prepared in manuscript.

Place	Date	Hour	Summary of Events and Information	Remarks and references to Appendices
RELLINGHEM	30.6.18		Strength of Officers & Other Ranks	
			34 916 Including Chaplain M.O. & Armr Sergt	
			23 687 Present with unit.	
			11 229 Detached from unit.	

J.W. Parr Lieut-Col
Comdg 26 Garr? Bn
Durham L.I.

2/6th Garrison Battalion Durham Light Infantry.

NOMINAL ROLL OF OFFICERS.

Lieut.Col.J.Spain.
Major G.Williams.
Captain T.Boddy.
Captain H.F.Hinde.
Captain W.H.C.Cooke.
Captain A.W.Lawton.
Captain G.R.Angus.
Hon.Capt.& QrMr J.E.Wiltshire.
Lieut.L.C.W.Benson.
Lieut.A.Green.
Lieut.A.Cook.
Lieut.W.G.Orriss.
Lieut.A.W.Drabble.
Lieut.F.Copeland.
Lieut.J.R.Wallace.
Lieut.F.G.Browne.
Lieut.C.J.A'Hern.
Lieut.J.E.Williamson.
Lieut.G.B.Howson.
2nd Lieut.W.S.Macadam.
2nd Lieut.R.Pratt.
2nd Lieut.L.H.Terry.
2nd Lieut.R.C.Montford.
2nd Lieut.L.V.Hardy.
2nd Lieut.S.B.Hodgson.
2nd Lieut.J.S.Willcox.
2nd Lieut.J.E.Smellie.
2nd Lieut.A.V.Blake.
2nd Lieut.C.St.A.Ratcliffe.
2nd Lieut.H.F.Lucas.
Lieut.H.V.Davis.
2nd Lieut.R.L.Davis.

30.6.1918.

Lieut.Colonel,
Commanding,
2/6th Gn.Bn.Durham L.I.

Confidential.

War Diary
of the
2/6th Bn Durham L.I.

for the month
of
July 1918.

WAR DIARY
INTELLIGENCE SUMMARY

Army Form C. 2118.

July 1918 pages 1 -
20th Bn Durham Light Infantry

Place	Date	Hour	Summary of Events and Information	Remarks and references to Appendices
RECLINGHEM	9.7.18		90290 Pte L. Elliott tried by F.G.C.M. for "Drunkenness" found guilty. Sentenced to 21 days F.P. No 1. Confirmed by Brig. Genl. C.M. James. Comdg. 177th Infty Bde.	Ref 5 heel
CANLERS	10.7.18		Battalion moved to CANLERS. K.7.a.5.3	7/B
	12.7.18		10. Officers reported. See nominal roll attached.	7/B
	15.7.18		99298 Pte (A/Cpl) H. J. Simmons tried by F.G.C.M. for "Drunkenness" found guilty. Sentenced to 14 days F.P. No 1. (automatically reverts to Pte) Confd. by Brig. Genl. C.M. James Comdg 177th Infty Bde. authy AG/2155/3853 (a) 27.6.17	7/B
	do.		The designation of unit is:- 76th Bn Durhks. authy:- WO letter 121/France/2110.(S.D.2). 8.7.18.	7/B
	17.7.18		Lt. 7 Copland, Lt. F.E. Williamson + Lt S.B. Hodgson having been examined by A.D.M.S. 59th Division & pronounced unfit for duty with unit, proceeded to Employment Base Depot. ETAPLES.	7/B
	20.7.18		11 unfit men to Base "E" Depot ETAPLES.	7/B
	22.7.18		38 unfit men to Base "E" Depot ETAPLES — eight returning to Force 3	7/B Sheet 44½
	21.7.18		A + C companies proceeded by bus to Q.11.d.6.9.a. to be attached to 11th Manchesters & 5th Dorsets in the line (front) for instruction. Orders cancelled at 11 pm. Returned to MAZINGARBE and rested in billets for the night. Returned by Bus to CANLERS. 7-10 pm. 22.7.18.	7/B
	23.7.18		Lieut. W. Macadam & Lt J.G. Browne having been examined by A.D.M.S. 59th Divn. Pronounced unfit for duty with unit, proceeded to Divl. Rest Camp with orders to report to Labour Corps Base Depot. BOULOGNE on 27th July, 1918.	7/B

July 1918. Part 2.
2/6th Durham L.I.

WAR DIARY
or
INTELLIGENCE SUMMARY.
(Erase heading not required.)

Army Form C. 2118.

Place.	Date	Hour	Summary of Events and Information	Remarks and references to Appendices
	1918 July			
CANLERS	24		18 men unfit to proceed up to front line owing to various disabilities were despatched to Divl Rest Camps.	6. C.B.
CHAT-	25		59th Divn became attached to 3rd Army VI Corps & moved up to the front area to relieve the 3rd Canadian Division in the line N of MERCATEL to BOISLEUX. No Bn. lent to 176th Bde for tactical Sker 51 SW.	6. C.B
MAIGRE			Proposed Disposition. 26th Bn R.Welsh Fus. [LEFT] 25th Bn Kings Liverpl Regt. [RIGHT] 2/6 Bn. in support at	
			CHAT MAIGRE relieving P.P.C.L.I. Square M.27 & 33.	do. do.
do	26		Quiet day in trenches except slight shelling 2.30 am 3.0 am & 4.5 pm & 6.30 pm 803444 Pte H G Edwards	6. C.B
			wounded severely in head by shrapnel. Progress made improvement of trenches.	do. do.
do	27/31		Quiet except for occasional shelling nightly at 10 pm & 2 am. do. do. do. do.	6. C.B
	30		Lieut. Col. Jos. SPAIN handed over command of Battalion to MAJOR. C.C. MESSERVY. after 1 year & 11 months service with the unit in that rank. {10th Worcr Regt.	6. C.B

STRENGTH Officers Other Ranks
              39.   833. including 8 Offrs 120 ORs. Detached.

Roll of Officers attached.

C. C. Messervy (Major Comdg. 2/6 Durham L.I.)

"2/6th Bn. Durham L.I.
Nominal Roll of Officers.

Major C.C. Messervy. Major G. Williams
Capt. J. Boddy. Capt. W.B. Wiltshire.
Capt. C.E. Molins. Med off Capt. N.P. Hinde.
Capt. G.R. Angus Capt. A.W. Lawton
Capt. W.H. Cooke Lieut. L.C. Benson.
Lieut. A. Green. Lieut. A. Cook
Lieut. W.G. Orviss. Lieut. A.W. Drabble
Lieut. F. Copeland Lieut. J.R. Wallace
Lieut. C.J.A. Hern. Lieut. F.V. Davis
Lieut. G.B. Howson. 2nd Lt. R. Pratt.
2nd Lt. L.N. Perry. 2nd Lt. R.C. Montford
2nd Lt. N.E. Brown. 2nd Lt. L.V. Hardy
2nd Lt. W.E. Scott. 2nd Lt. R. Black.
2nd Lt. J.S. Willcox 2nd Lt. R.W. Flintoff
2nd Lt. R.A. Davis 2nd Lt. J.E. Smellie
Lieut. H.S. Sitwell 2nd Lt. W.A.D. Connelley
2nd Lt. D. Allen. 2nd Lt. A.B. Blake
2nd Lt. H.F. Lucas 2nd Lt. C.H.A. Ratcliffe
2nd Lt. G.W. McDonagh 2nd Lt. P.S. Lund.
2nd Lt. C.E.M. Smith

31.7.1918.
C.C. Messervy
Major
Comdg. 2/6 Durh. L.I.

172/59 WL4

Confidential

War Diary

of the

2/6th Bn Durham Light Infantry

for the month

of

August 1918.

2/6th Dh. Duh: L.I.

WAR DIARY
INTELLIGENCE SUMMARY

August 1918. page 1

Place	Date	Hour	Summary of Events and Information	Remarks and references to Appendices
CHAT MAIGRE	1.8.18		LIEUT. C.J.A'HERN struck off strength & remains attached as Adjt. 59th Divl. Regtl. Camp. with effect 26.6.18	C.C.B
	1.8.18		A/MAJOR. E.A. ASH 5th Middlesex Regt. (S.R.) arrived 31.7.18 & took over Command of Battalion with rank of Lt. Col. with effect 1.8.18.	
"			QMR & Hon. LIEUT. F.A.S. BERRY (late 25th York Regt.) arrived 31.7.18.	
"			LIEUT. F. COPELAND. 6th D.L.I. having been found fit reported from Base 30.7.18	C.C.B
"	3.8.18		Relieved in trenches by 11th Bn. S.L.I. to Bde. Reserve at BRETENCOURT.	C.C.B
BRETENCOURT	4.8.18		A/MAJOR. H. G. WILLIAMS left unit. (med unfit). to 3rd Army as Town Major.	C.C.B
"	5.8.18		A/MR & Hon CAPT. W.B WILTSHIRE left unit, for Pool of Offrs. CALAIS. (med unfit)	C.C.B
"	5.8.18		2ND LIEUTS. W.E. MARWOOD. B. GASH. W. WATKIN. arrived	C.C.B
"	6.8.18		LIEUT. G.B. HOWSON. 2ND LIEUT. R.C. MONTFORD off strength to BASE DEPOT ETAPLES. (med unfit)	C.C.B
"	7.8.18		79477 Pte J. DUNKLEY committed suicide by shooting himself.	S.I.9.S.E.C.C.B
"	7.8.18		Occupied battle position in PURPLE RESERVE R.35.c.6.4. PRACTICE.	C.C.B
"	8.8.18		to Divisional Reserve GOUY EN ARTOIS.	C.C.B
GOUY-EN-ARTOIS	11.6.18		2ND LT. T. CLARK arrived	C.C.B
"	13.8.18		MAJOR. C.C. MESSERY. (Here Regt.) to Base Depot ETAPLES. (med unfit)	C.C.B
"	14.8.18		CAPT. T. BODDY. ADJT. to Hospital 21st C.C.S struck off strength 23.8.18 to England	C.C.B

WAR DIARY or INTELLIGENCE SUMMARY

Army Form C. 2118.

August 1916. Page 2.

Place	Date	Hour	Summary of Events and Information	Remarks and references to Appendices
GOUY-en-ARTOIS	14		MAJOR. H.C. CANNON QUEEN'S REG^T reports his arrival as 2nd in Command.	6. C. B
"	15		2/LT. T. CLARK to Hospital.	6. C. B
"	15		Inspection by V11th CORPS COMMANDER. LIEUT GEN. HALDANE. K.C.G. D.S.O. Sir A	6. C. B
"	16, 17		Training including L.G. Signalling &c.	6. C. B
MERCATEL	17		Relieved 11th R. Scot. Fusiliers in MERCATEL, BOISLEUX, ST MARC front line.	6. C. B
"	18		Patrol sent out to ascertain if enemy occupied LONG ALLEY - SUMP TRENCH - SPINNEY AVENUE - RESULT. No Signs of enemy.	6. C. B
"	19		Enemy M.G. Emplacements located S6B # 2 - 6.	6. C. B
"	20		Same ground as 18th & 19th patrolled, no enemy seen.	6. C. B
"	22		Posts (advanced) established at S6^c. 9.7, S6^d.1.6. S6^c.8.5.10. Enemy located at S12.2.9. + CRUCIFIX.	6. C. B
"	23	5 am	52nd Scottish Division attacked through our lines with good results, advancing about 2½ Kilometres. Prisoners came freely into the line soon after barrage started. Casualties slight.	6. C. B
"			Battalion withdrew to SAULTY at NOON. 23rd bivouacked for night.	
SAULTY			Moved by rail to AIRE + route march to LAMBRES.	6. C. B
LAMBRES	24		Moved by bus to ST VENANT ASYLUM. Enemy shells LADEN with H.V. shells during night, no casualties.	6. C. B
ST VENANT	26			6. C. B

Army Form C. 2118.

2/6/1 page 3

WAR DIARY
or
INTELLIGENCE SUMMARY
for August 1918

(Erase heading not required.)

Instructions regarding War Diaries and Intelligence Summaries are contained in F. S. Regs., Part II. and the Staff Manual respectively. Title pages will be prepared in manuscript.

Place	Date	Hour	Summary of Events and Information	Remarks and references to Appendices
CALONNE	27.8.18		59th Divn. relieved 74th Divn. in line on MERVILLE Sector. 2/6th D.L.I. relieving 14th Royal Highlanders in support	36.A. G.C.S.
do	29.8.18		11th S.L.I. Right Batl. of Bde. 15th Essex Left.	G.C.S.
			Enemy heavily shelled. 3 killed. 3 wounded.	G.C.S.
L'EPINETTE	30.8.18		2/6 D.L.I. relieved 11th S.L.I. The 177th Bde. advance their line.	
NEAR LESTREM	31.8.18		Line advanced from Road running N&S through A.21.c & A.9." to line running N&S from	36.A. S.E.
			R.12.c.4.4. to R.24.c.3.0. enemy's rearguard patrols of machine guns very active	1 - 29 000 G.C.S.
			Bn. H.Q. R.13.d.3.r.	
			Strength 36 Officers 789 Other Ranks.	

Ernest A. Ash—
Lieut Col.
Commdg. 2/6th Durham L.I.

T2134. Wt. W708-776. 500000. 4/15. Sir J. C. & S.

WAR DIARY

2/5th Bn. Durham Light Infantry — Army Form C. 2118.

September 1918.

INTELLIGENCE SUMMARY.
(Erase heading not required.)

Place	Date	Hour	Summary of Events and Information	Remarks and references to Appendices
	Sept.			
RIVER LAYE	1/2nd		Occupied position HUITS MAISONS POST – R.23.d.7.0. – BOUT DEVILLE POST – R.24.d.4.L – R.17.d.20.9.m. – LE MARAIS	Sheet 36a
near LESTREM			E. POST – R.M.S.I enduring sharp fighting but position consolidated with casualties. 6 killed & 20 wounded, including & killed Capt. A.H.C. COOKE 1/5th Bn. KORL att'd 2/6 D.L.I. wounded Capt. R.M. LAWTON	
			4th Bn. N.F. BROWN 2/6 D.L.I. Lt. Col. E.A. ASH & the unit congratulated on good work by	
			MAJ. GEN. SMYTH. Comdg 59th Division. 5 Military Medals since awarded in connection with operation	
do	2		176 Bde in support relieved by 178 Bde	
ROBECQ	3		To reserves P.22.d. 9.0. 50.	
PARADIS	5		Moved forward as Division advancing	
FOSSE	7		do	
Rt. BAILLEUL	9		Relieved 178th Bde in CORPS MAIN BATTLE AREA.	MAP AUBERS
M.17.c. S.4.	13		Relieved 1st R. Sussex Regt. in OUTPOST SYSTEM	
LA BASSE Rd.	19		In Brigade Support	
CLIFTON C. POST	22		In Brigade Reserve on relief by 178th Bde	
			In to line relieving 11th R. Scots fus. 176th Bde.	
NINE PIN TRENCH	29		The following men have been awarded the "Military Medal" for gallantry & devotion to duty in the Field.	
			74606 Pte J. Clark. 22232 Pte B. Benson. 301410 Pte Jeffries W.H. 79603. Pte Robinson A.B. 6362. Pte Green A.	

Army Form C. 2118.

WAR DIARY
or
INTELLIGENCE SUMMARY.
(Erase heading not required.)

September 1918
9/t Bn Durham L.I.
Pg 2

Instructions regarding War Diaries and Intelligence Summaries are contained in F. S. Regs., Part II. and the Staff Manual respectively. Title pages will be prepared in manuscript.

Place	Date	Hour	Summary of Events and Information	Remarks and references to Appendices
			The undermentioned Officers have joined at left during September 1918.	
	During 2nd		Lt. W. Woodward.	
	do		3rd. 2/Lt R.P. Latham	
	do		4th Lieut. J. Blyth.	
	do		Rev. J.W. Hall. (Chaplain)	
			Reinforcements. Losses.	
			11th 15 10 Killed.	
			20th 12 35 Wounded.	
			25th 4 106 Struck off. (over 7 days hosp.)	
			2nd 78	
			Strength. 30.9.18.	
	do	24	Capt. J. Stephenson Adjutant	
	do		27th. Lt. L. Watson.	
			Actual figure of Strength 29/9/18. Officers. 40.
			Capt. A.W. Lawler. do 17/9/18. Other Ranks. 791.
			Lieut. N.S. Brown do 26/9/18.	
			2/Lieut. C.E.M. Smith do 29/9/18.	
			Capt. 10/R. Cooke do 14/9/18.	
				W. Currie Major
				Comdg 9/6 Bn Durh. L.I.

Army Form C. 2118.

2/6th Bn Durham L.J.

WAR DIARY

INTELLIGENCE SUMMARY

OCTOBER 1918.

No 6

Instructions regarding War Diaries and Intelligence Summaries are contained in F.S. Regs., Part II. and the Staff Manual respectively. Title pages will be prepared in manuscript.

(Erase heading not required.)

Place	Date	Hour	Summary of Events and Information	Remarks and references to Appendices
	1918			
NEAR AUBERS	Oct. 1		Line pushed forward to TILLELOY. N. POST – WINCHESTER POST – M.23.4.4.4. "D" Coy in line. B.H.Q. ELGIN POST.	AUBERS SHEET 36 N.W.
AUBERS	2		D & B Coys again advanced. B & D Coys penetrated enemy's lines of previous day to a depth of 5 Kilos without getting into touch with him. 59th Division relieved by 47th Division, the London Irish taking over 2/6 D.L.I. frontage, this unit withdrawing to BOUTDEVILLE.	
LILLE	3		Proceeded by lorry & march route to CROIX MARECHAL relieving 2/4 D.B.L.I.	36 N.E.
SECTOR	4/6		Continuous gentle advance. Bn. H.Q. M24.f.1.2. (GUNNERS WALK). Received message from CORPS Comdr. Congratulating unit on good work during previous week Bde Comdr adding following "The DLI have done uncommonly well".	
CROIX MARECHAL	7		Relieved by Essex Regt. withdrew to CROIX MARECHAL.	
BAC ST MAUR	10/13		177th Bde in Divisional Rest. TRAINING.	
	14		XIst CORPS COMDR presented ribbons of the MILITARY MEDAL to the following :- 252790. Sergt TOWERS C. 99256. Pte HARKER H. 74646 Pte CLARK T. 22832. Pte BENSON B. 301410. Pte JEFFRIES. W.H. 79603. Pte RICHARDSON A.E. 64362. Pte GREEN A.	
CROIX MARECHAL	16		Moved into Bde reserve.	
CARINGHEM	17		The advance continued.	
ST ANDRE ST MAURICE	18		Entered the suburbs of LILLE. Received everywhere by the inhabitants with great rejoicing.	

Army Form C. 2118.

2/10th Bn Durham L.I.

WAR DIARY

INTELLIGENCE SUMMARY.

October 1918. Page 2.

(Erase heading not required.)

Instructions regarding War Diaries and Intelligence Summaries are contained in F. S. Regs., Part II. and the Staff Manual respectively. Title pages will be prepared in manuscript.

Place	Date	Hour	Summary of Events and Information	Remarks and references to Appendices
LILLE SECTOR	Oct/18.		The houses in all the streets decorated with French allied flags. A noticeable feature on this day was the fact of it being the first time for months the unit had entered a town or village without finding houses wrecked by shell fire or mine. The spirit of the 2/10 D.L.I. this day was something to be proud of, marching a distance of 17 kilos , singing practically the whole of the distance.	SHEET 37/.
LE RECUEIL	19		Moved forward to LE RECUEIL.	
TOUFFLEURS	20/21		,, ,, to TOUFFLEURS. & rested till 22nd	
RIVER ESCAUT (SCHELDT.)	22		Into front line relieving 19th King's Liverpools on RIVER ESCAUT Battalion Frontage. I.2.b central to I.8. central to I.8. Central. Bn HQrs Chateau I.10.b.4.2. The enemy holding the Right bank of the river except for 1 machine gun post which had been established by King's Lpool's. The ground on the RIGHT Bank of the River is a breadth of about 1/2 kilo is very flat & marshy, several feet of water standing thereon in many places, it then rises to MONT DE LA TRINITE which is surmounted by a CHURCH and provides excellent observation, the slopes of the mountain are well wooded & the further side of same holds the enemy Artillery, the nearer side being defended by trench overlain & M.G. posts, which appear to be situated along the HERRINES railway which runs along the foot	

Army Form C. 2118.

WAR DIARY
or
INTELLIGENCE SUMMARY.
(Erase heading not required.)

2/6th Bn K.L.I. October 1918. Page 3.

Place	Date	Hour	Summary of Events and Information	Remarks and references to Appendices
SCHELDT	29/30		There are only 2 tracks which can be used & a frontal attack presents many difficulties in view of the nature of ground; however, despite all this, one company has been established on the right bank of the river & continual touch kept with the enemy. Aerial activity well maintained & counter battery work above normal. Headqrs being heavily shelled on many occasions. Casualties during 29/30 Oct. 6 killed. 16 wounded all other ranks	Sheet 37
	30		Relieved by the 11th S.L.I.	
HULANS	31		Brigade Reserve.	

Ernest A. Ash
Lieut Colonel
Commanding 2/6th Bn Durham L.I.

Army Form C. 2118.

2/6th Bn Durham L.I.   October 1918.

WAR DIARY
INTELLIGENCE SUMMARY

(Erase heading not required.)

page #

Place	Date	Hour	Summary of Events and Information	Remarks and references to Appendices
HONOURS & DECORATIONS			The following awards have been made during the month for Gallantry & Devotion to Duty.	
			MILITARY CROSS. 2/Lt. L.H. PERRY. (4th Gloucester Regt) attached 2/6 D.L.I. 4.X.18.	
			MILITARY MEDALS. 54636. Sergt P.J. Spragg; 252651. Cpl. R. Russell; 302671. L/Cpl. R.B. Bailey; 74831. Pte. W. Kohler; 99241. Pte. A. Siverski; 99190. Pte. J. Cowburn; 294617. Pte. W. Pashley. } 17.X.18	
			857745. Pte. W. Jeffries. 252468. Pte. A. Richardson. 4.X.18.	
			252790. Sergt. G. Towers; 99256. Pte. H. Harker. 8.X.18.	
			252534. Cpl. J.R. Mills. 33128. L/Cpl. J.N. Cawthorn: 76368. Pte. A. Dowling.	
STRENGTH			Officers	
			Decrease { 2nd Lieut R.P. Lattimer. Wounded. 2.X.18. to England 13.X.18.	
			do R.L. Davis do 6.X.18	
			do L.H. Perry. M.C. Killed in action 6.X.18.	
			do W.A.D. Connelley. off strength. 4.X.18 (Med. Bd. England)	
			Increase { do G. McVicker 9.X.18	
			do H.A. Stedman. 10.X.18	
			do L.H. Knightsall 10.X.18	
			Capt. J. Turnbull. attached for 1 month. 25.X.18	
31.X.18			Officers 36 attached 3	
			Other Ranks. 729	

Ernest A. Ash. Lieut. Col.
Commanding 2/6 Bn Durham L.I.

No. WS 33
Date 2/12/18
2/6th R. Dub. L.I.

WAR DIARY
or
INTELLIGENCE SUMMARY

NOVEMBER 1918

Army Form C. 2118.

Place	Date Nov/18	Hour	Summary of Events and Information	Remarks and references to Appendices
HUKANS.	1		In Brigade Reserve.	
VERMELLES (Haye)	3		Into the line relieving 15th Essex Regt. frontage I.26.b central to I.20 central.	Sheet 39.
	3/8		Work consisted mainly of patrols with object of keeping close touch with enemy who was believed to be preparing for a withdrawal on large scale. Enemy very active with T.Ms M.G's + Artillery.	
	"8		Relieved by 11th R. Scots Fusiliers into reserve at TOUFFLEURS	
TOUFFLERS	8/10		The enemy having withdrawn on night 9/10, the 59th Division commenced to press forward the 2/6 Br. I. being ordered to proceed to GOUDINIERS J.19. on arrival at PECQ, however found bridge at I.2 central had given way owing to numbers of troops guns re passing across. Later ordered to return to RUMEZ as 177th Brigade no longer required to continue pursuit. The enemy being hard pressed by divisions on Right + left tomorrow js.	
RUMEZ	11			
RUMEZ	11	1100	Notice received that the enemy has been granted an ARMISTICE by Gen'l FOCH on terms which were practically "unconditional surrender". The Bat's band played both the English & French "Belgian" National Anthems at 11.00 hrs. and at 12.00 a Thanksgiving Service was held.	
TEMPLEUVE	12		Moved into Billets better suited for comfort of troops.	

Army Form C. 2118.

WAR DIARY
or
INTELLIGENCE SUMMARY.
(Erase heading not required.)

2/c An/Shl November 18 Page 2.

Place	Date Nov/18	Hour	Summary of Events and Information	Remarks and references to Appendices
ASCQ	15		Billets for night en route to LILLE area. The unit is now transferred with the Division to FIRST ARMY.	Maps. TOURNAI K.1.
SECLIN	16.		To SECLIN by Route march via SAINGHIN - PERONNE - FASTIN - AVELIN.	K.8.
	16/30.		Light training, Sports. Concert &c. also bi-weekly trips to GONDECOURT Cinema, with the opportunity of flights re. Daily Bus Runs to LILLE & WO's, NCO's & Men's Club which has been opened by Division.	A.
			The following have been awarded the MILITARY MEDAL for Gallantry & Devotion to Duty in the Field. 252445 Pte W.H. BARNES. 65798. Sgt. R. HANCOCK. 350860 Pte W. COOK.	
			2/Lt A. WARDLE awaits MILITARY CROSS. for Gallantry & Devotion to Duty in the Field.	B.
STRENGTH.			OFFICERS. INCREASE. 30 Nov 18. Officers 42	
			2nd Lt B.G. Sharp. 3rd D.L.I.	3
			Capt G Williams. 9th Yorks	Other Ranks 767
			Lt (A/Capt) T.W. Liddell M.C. 2nd D.L.I.	
			Capt R.E. Oliver. 1st Bn (S). Scot. Rifles	
			Capt S.A.O. Baddeley. 6th Middlesex	
			Lieut T.H. Miller. 6th D.L.I.	
19			2/Lt T.W. Given. do	
27			E.A. Pickering. do	
			DECREASE. Nov 1 2/Lt A.W. Blake. England, sick. Date 2/Lt R.C. Davis. do wounded. Nov 11 Capt/ P. Heide. Med Board, England	
			Ernest A. Ash. Lieut Col. Commdg 1/6th Bn. Durh. L.I.	

Confidential

War Diary
of the
2/6th Battalion the Durham Light Infantry
for the
month of
December 1918.

Army Form C. 2118.

2/6th Durham L.I. WAR DIARY DECEMBER 1918.

INTELLIGENCE SUMMARY
(Erase heading not required.)

Instructions regarding War Diaries and Intelligence Summaries are contained in F. S. Regs., Part II. and the Staff Manual respectively. Title pages will be prepared in manuscript.

Place	Date 1918 Dec	Hour	Summary of Events and Information	Remarks and references to Appendices
SECLIN. near LILLE.	1/7		Battalion did one hour's military training and two hour's educational training each morning, Sports in the afternoon.	
	3		Regimental sports. 2 prizes in each event value of prizes varying from 15 Frs to 55 Frs.	
			17 Events brought keen competition & a good day's sport was the result.	
BRACQUEMONT.	7		Moved by Motor bus to occupied Australian Camp ARCQUEMONT near NOEUX-les-MINES.	
	7/31		Work for period. Education, practically the whole of Battalion taking part either as students or teachers.	
			SALVAGE. A great deal of work done in this connection with good results.	
			Frequent concerts by Battalion troupe & Band. also by other units of Division.	
	8		Presentation of Decorations by Major Genl N.M. Smyth VC. CB. Div Comdr. The under mentioned were the recipients of the ribbons:-	
			D.C.M. 66693. Pte MURPHY. J. MILITARY MEDALS. 252651. Cpl. RUSSELL. R.	
			M.M. 25253H. Cpl. MILLS J.A. 302671. L/Cpl BAILEY. R.B. 74831. Pte KOHLER. W. 301410. Pte JEFFREYS. W.H.	
			358850. Pte COOK. W. 99190. Pte COWBURN. F. 76368. Pte DOWLING. A. 294617. Pte PASHLEY. W.	
			79603. Pte RICHARDSON. A.E. 252442. Pte BARNES. W.H. 99241 Pte SNIGARSKI. A. 33118 L/Cpl CAWTHORN. J.	
			The undermentioned officer has been awarded BAR. to.THE. MILITARY CROSS.	
			2nd LIEUT. A. WARDLE, M.C., Corps Routine Order dated 4.12.18.	
			— OVER —	

Army Form C. 2118.

2/5th Durham L.I. WAR DIARY December 1918.

INTELLIGENCE SUMMARY. page 2.

(Erase heading not required.)

Place	Date	Hour	Summary of Events and Information	Remarks and references to Appendices
BRACQUEMONT	Dec 25		A very good X'mas dinner was arranged for all other ranks, consisting of Roast Pork, Brussels Sprouts, Potatoes &, Plum Pudding, Mince Pies, Fruit, Oranges, Nuts &, Cigarettes & Beer. General remarks by the men that the dinner was excellent.	
			Officers. Decrease.	
			Capt. G.R. Angus. To England Sick. 24-11-18.	
			2 Lt. T. Clark. do do 23.11.18.	
			Increase.	
			2nd Lieut Le Tunnell. 25.11.18.	Strength 31.12.18
				Officers. 42 (including attached)
				Other Ranks. 700.
			Ernest G. Ash	
			Lieut Colonel	
			Commanding 2/5th Bn Durham Light Infantry	

Confidential

No. 1 Sir 2/7th Bn. Durham L.I. January 1919

Army Form C. 2118.

WAR DIARY or **INTELLIGENCE SUMMARY**
(Erase heading not required.)

Instructions regarding War Diaries and Intelligence Summaries are contained in F.S. Regs., Part II. and the Staff Manual respectively. Title pages will be prepared in manuscript.

Place	Date January 1919	Hour	Summary of Events and Information	Remarks and references to Appendices
GRAEQUEMONT	1/15		Work Consists of SALVAGE & EDUCATION.	
	3		Demobilisation commenced.	
ST MARTIN EGLISE	15/17		Moved to Demobilisation Camp DIEPPE	
DIEPPE			Unit called upon to provide all our Camp duties elsewhere so Gradual demobilization of the place rather comes to a late date, chiefly from for the demobilization of drafts from other units attached to 100th Batt. (also to this Service) but remains in 177th Batt. Adv. for all other Services.	
			Demobilised during month —	
			Officers — 10 Other Ranks — 119	
			Officers	DIEPPE					
			Major G.W. Heslop med. Board England 27.12.18 (not)	
			Capt. G. Wilson med. Board England 14.12.18 (not)	
			Lieut W. Allen " " " 7.1.19 (not)	
			2nd Lt. J. Donald " England Ord. 9.1.19	
			2nd Lt. C.P. Robson " " " 20.1.19	
				Strength 31st January 1919	
				Officers 38 (including attached)
			2nd Lt. J.W. Dyson Demobilised 31.1.19	Other Ranks 549
			Officers Arrived	
			Lieut (Q.Mr.) R.S. Manuel R.A. Arrived 21.1.19	
			" " " do do 24.1.19	
			Lieut (A/Capt) L. Marten	

Ernest A. Ash
Lieut-Colonel
Commanding 2/7 B. The Durham Light Infantry

CONFIDENTIAL

Vol 10

2/6th Battalion The Durham Light Infantry

WAR DIARY

FOR THE MONTH OF

FEBRUARY 1919

Army Form C. 2118.

1/6th Durham Light Infantry. WAR DIARY February 1919.

INTELLIGENCE SUMMARY

(Erase heading not required.)

Instructions regarding War Diaries and Intelligence Summaries are contained in F.S. Regs., Part II. and the Staff Manual respectively. Title pages will be prepared in manuscript.

Place	Date	Hour	Summary of Events and Information	Remarks and references to Appendices
Martin Eglise Embarkation Camp.	February 1-28.		Battalion accommodated in huts in "D" Block. Responsible for the working of the Dépôt. Gradual demobilization of the Battalion continued. Numbers demobilized during the month :- Officers : 2. (Capt. J. Turnbull and Lieut. A.J. Lucas). Other ranks : 162.	
	13.		Capt. J. Elliston departed for duty, and taken on Strength of Battalion.	
	18.		Capt. T.W. Hall, C.F., left the Battalion, and proceeded to the 2nd Division, II Army, for duty.	
	28.		Strength of Battalion :- Officers : 36. Other ranks : 346.	

Ernest O. Ash. Lt. Col.
Commdg. 1/6th Bn. the Durham Light Infantry.

2/6TH.BN.THE DURHAM LIGHT INFANTRY.

NOMINAL ROLL OF OFFICERS.

Lt-Col. E.A.Ashb
Major H.C.Cannon, M.C.
Captain J.Stephenson, M.C.
Captain R.E.Oliver.
Captain A.W.Liddell, M.C.
Captain F.J.Blythe,
Captain W.Watkin.
Captain W.Woodward.
Captain F.Gilbertson.
Captain J.C.Avellone, M.O.R.C., U.S. (Attached)
Lieut L.C.A.Benson.
Lieut A.Cook.
Lieut W.G.Orriss.
Lieut A.W.Drabble.
Lieut E.Asbrey.
Lieut T.H.Miller.
Lieut J.S.Willcox.
Lieut H.S.Sitwell.
Lieut F.Copeland.
Lieut L.Martin.
Lieut R.H.Stewart.
2nd.Lt.R.Pratt.
2ndLt.W.E.Marwood.
2nd.Lt.A.Wardle, M.C.
2nd.Lt.G.McVicker.
2nd.Lt.R.W.Flintoff.
2nd.Lt.W.Osborne.
2nd.Lt.S.C.Watson.
2nd.Lt.R.Black.
2nd.Lt.L.V.Hardy.
2nd.Lt.J.E.Smellie.
2nd.Lt.E.G.Sharp.
2nd.Lt.G.W,McDonagh.
2nd.Lt.G.Jeffreys.
2nd.Lt.H.A.Stedman.
2nd.Lt.H.A.Stedman.

CONFIDENTIAL.

2/6th Battalion The Durham Light Infantry

WAR DIARY

FOR THE

MONTH OF MARCH 1919.

HEADQUARTERS
S.R.14/25?
1 - APR 1919
177th INFANTRY BRIGADE

Army Form C. 2118.

WAR DIARY
or
~~INTELLIGENCE~~ SUMMARY. March 1919.
(Erase heading not required.)

Instructions regarding War Diaries and Intelligence Summaries are contained in F.S. Regs., Part II. and the Staff Manual respectively. Title pages will be prepared in manuscript.

Place	Date	Hour	Summary of Events and Information	Remarks and references to Appendices
Martin-Eglise	1-13.		Battalion at Martin-Eglise Embarkation Camp. Responsible for the running of the Selones.	
	14.	1600.	Battalion entrained at Arques-la-Bataille station. Train left at 2130 hours.	
	15.	1130.	Battalion detrained at Matquise - Rincent station (near Calais). Marched to No. 34 P.O.W. Camp. Beaurieu.	
BEAURIEU	15.			
	15-22.		Battalion furnished guards to Nos. 35, 36, 74, 34, 92 and 101 P.O.W. Companies. These escorts were sent to Chief Inspection P.O.W. Companies, there entirely detached from the Battalion.	
	21.		One Company (7 Officers & 259 other ranks) proceeded to Military Prison, Vendroux, near Calais, to furnish guards there.	
CALAIS.	22.		Remainder of Battalion moved by march-route to No. 7 Camp, Calais.	
	23-31.		Battalion responsible for furnishing guards at East & West Docks, Bakeries, R.A.O.C., Valdelièvre, I.P. Compound, Les Baraques &c.	
	15-31.		Large drafts arrived from the 17th, 18th, 24th Durham L.I., also from 15th Yorks & Lancs Regt.	
	31.		Battalion strength :- Officers : 45. Other ranks : 1080.	

Ernest A. Oak Lt. Col.
Commdg. 19th Durham Light Infantry.

CONFIDENTIAL.

2/6th Btn: The Durham Light Infantry.

Vol 12

WAR DIARY

FOR THE MONTH OF

APRIL, 1919.

Army Form C. 2118.

WAR DIARY
or
INTELLIGENCE SUMMARY
April 1919.

(Erase heading not required.)

Place	Date	Hour	Summary of Events and Information	Remarks and references to Appendices
CALAIS.	1-30.		Battalion at No.7 Camp, CALAIS. Responsible for furnishing guards & escorts at East & West Docks, and stations & other places in the CALAIS area.	
	30.		Strength of Battalion:— Officers: 41. Other Ranks: 1112.	

Ernest A. Ada? Lt-Col.
Commandg 70th Bn. The Durham Light Infantry.

CONFIDENTIAL

2/10th Bn. The Durham Light Infantry Vol 13

WAR DIARY

FOR THE MONTH OF

MAY 1919.

Army Form C. 2118.

WAR DIARY
~~INTELLIGENCE SUMMARY~~
(Erase heading not required.)

May 1919.

Instructions regarding War Diaries and Intelligence Summaries are contained in F.S. Regs., Part II. and the Staff Manual respectively. Title pages will be prepared in manuscript.

Place	Date	Hour	Summary of Events and Information	Remarks and references to Appendices
Calais.	1-3.		Battalion drill at No. 7 Camp, and responsible for furnishing guards on docks &c. in Calais.	
	6.		"A" Coy. moved to Val-de-Lièvre, and took over guard duties from the North Lond. Regt. at the Ordnance Depôt. Motor-Charabanc runs for Officers & O.R. on Saturdays during the months to places of interest in the battle area.	
			Lt.-Col. J.W. Fetherbridge R.T.O. assumed Command of the Battalion, vice Lt. Col. E.A. Robb who proceeded to Winchester for repatriation.	
	10.		Training as follows on 2nd day off Guard-duties:— 3/4 hr. Lewis Gun or Signal Training. " " P.G. Games. " " Rifle Exercises; Saluting Drill; Guard Mounting Drill; Marching Past.	

Lt. Cormurtz. [signed]
Commdg. 12th Bn. the Durham L.I.

Army Form C. 2118.

WAR DIARY
or
~~INTELLIGENCE SUMMARY.~~
(Erase heading not required.)

June 1919.

Place	Date	Hour	Summary of Events and Information	Remarks and references to Appendices
No. 7 Camp. Calais.	1-29.		Battalion at Calais. Responsible for furnishing guards to the duties in Calais.	
	24.		Day observed as a holiday in honour of the signing of the Peace. At night the men had a dance.	
	27.		Men had their peace dinner.	
	29-30.		Battalion moved into Nos. 4, 5 & 1st Camps, and relieved the 15th Bn. the Essex Regt. who took over the duties in the No. 7 Camp.	
	30.		Strength:— Officers:— 29. + 1 R.A.C.D + 1 Ass. Educn. Officer. Other Ranks:— 977.	

K. Cameron Major.
Commdg. 16th Durham L. I.

WAR DIARY
or
INTELLIGENCE SUMMARY

Army Form C. 2118.

2/6 D.L.I.
July 1919.

Place	Date	Hour	Summary of Events and Information	Remarks and references to Appendices
Nos. 4, 5 and 8 Leave Camps Calais.	1-31.		Battalions responsible for the running of the 3 Leave Camps.	
	6.		Massed Church Parade (Thanksgiving Service in honor of Peace) at No. 7 Camp.	
	14.		Peace celebrations in Place d'Armes, Calais. This unit supplied 6 officers and 100 men. The following congratulatory letters were received:—	
			1. From Brig. Genl. J.H.Hall, Commanding 177th Infty. Bde.	
			"Please convey to all Officers, NCO's men of your Battalion who took part in the French Peace Celebration Parade, my appreciation of their exceptional turn-out, smartness & steadiness. They showed themselves worthy representatives of the Brigade throughout the proceedings."	
			2. From Brig. Genl. F. S. Rogan, Base Commandant, Calais.	
			"I wish to express my appreciation of the turn-out and drill of your Company at the Review yesterday. Your Battalion is noted for its smartness of turn-out and handling of arms, and the Company yesterday fully maintained the Battalion's reputation, and that of the distinguished regiment to which it belongs. The presence of such a unit in Calais is of great assistance in upholding the prestige of the British Army, a matter of no small moment nowadays."	
			3. From Genl. Fitt, Governor of Calais.	
			"The Review held on the occasion of the celebration of the French National Fête and of the victory for which you have been so good enough to provide a detachment from the troops under your orders, is afresh proof of the 'Solidarité'"	

2.

Army Form C. 2118.

WAR DIARY
or
INTELLIGENCE SUMMARY

(Erase heading not required.)

July 1919. (continued).

Place	Date	Hour	Summary of Events and Information	Remarks and references to Appendices
			of the British Army." Thanksgiving for once again having Emphasised our brotherhood in arms. They up the so good as to bring to the notice of the troops who attended the parade, my warmest congratulations on their first turn-out and soldier-like bearing."	
	19.		Whole holiday in honour of the signing of Peace. Aquatic sports on the lagoon during the afternoon. Dances and fireworks at night.	
	31.		Amount invested in War Savings Cetifs. during the month: 4691.80 Francs. 166 Certificates bought.	
			Strength: Officers: 32 + 2 attached. Other Ranks: 964.	

J. W. dellVraag Lt.Col.
Commdg. York & Durham L.I.

177 Bde.

Army Form C. 2118.

WAR DIARY
or
~~INTELLIGENCE SUMMARY~~ August 1919.

(Erase heading not required.)

Instructions regarding War Diaries and Intelligence Summaries are contained in F. S. Regs., Part II. and the Staff Manual respectively. Title pages will be prepared in manuscript.

Place	Date	Hour	Summary of Events and Information	Remarks and references to Appendices
Vendroux	3.		"A" Coy moved to Vendroux.	
	5.		"D" " " " "	
			"B" Hqrs. moved to Cologne Camp.	
			"B" responsible for furnishing guards & escorts in the Vendroux area.	
	29.		"B" moved from Cologne and Vendroux to No. 6 Camp, Calais.	
	31.		83 Derby men demobilised during the month.	
			Strength of Bn :— Officers : 28.	
			Other Ranks : 900.	

J. W. Lethbridge Lt. Col.
Comndg. /6th Durham L.I.

[Orderly Room stamp: 6th Bn. Durham Light Infantry]

www.ingramcontent.com/pod-product-compliance
Lightning Source LLC
Chambersburg PA
CBHW081456160426
43193CB00013B/2506